THE
SEEKER

THE
SEEKER

Lost Lyrics and Poems
of Fleeting Violet

PALMETTO
PUBLISHING
Charleston, SC
www.PalmettoPublishing.com

Copyright © 2024 by Fleeting Violet

All rights reserved

Hardcover ISBN: 979-8-8229-4205-9
Paperback ISBN: 979-8-8229-4206-6

CONTENTS

Dedicated to those who are my light.
Thank you for standing beside me and
ushering me into a new era in my life.
This book is yours as much as it is mine.
Love you.

A Pacifist's Parable

Was it worth it?
I watched you burn it down
An accomplice
That you just kept around

The monster you fight
Is a god in disguise
Telling you to stop
And go home

I pleaded and cried
Almost every single night
Can you look me in the eye
When you light it up?

Was it worth it?
When you dragged me down
I stayed sick from being someone
You kept around

You think power and glory
Make you the hero in the story
But you left no one to tell

I can see you lost your mind
If you seek, you will find
But can you look me in the eye
When you light it up?

Projections

I was what I thought
You said to me
You dreamed up
In some fantasy
A projected idea
On a movie screen

"Thought you'd rather
Be with some
Bro-type, all-American"
Well, you must not
Know me very well

See, I was never the cool kid
Never the girl people wanted
Tried to prove that I was
worth something

I spend most of my time
Atop a pedestal in someone's mind
A false answer to your insecurities
That bring out all of mine
But I'm just a mirror
I mirror what you wanna see

I wear a mask to mask the things
I don't want you to know
When it gradually seeps out,
I freak out
Begging for your approval
I turn my pain into a sideshow
As long as they're laughing, they
need you
Isn't that how it goes?

There are layers to your pain
The origin and how you
cope with everything
Soon, it gets buried in your
mind's grave
Your past becomes a statuesque
figurine
I memorialized a girl I used to
know
Thinking becoming someone else
Would make me forget
But it just makes me feel more
alone

So I wait
For a person, a place, or a moment
To unfreeze the girl who is unafraid
But I pray for a chance
That I won't need any of
those things

Pedestal

You said I need to grow up
Do you know what that means?
You've got your list of problems
And now you've added me

Maybe I need to grow up
It's probably overdue
Pushing thirty in a dream
And I don't wanna come to

You call me up sometimes
I don't know what to say
There are no words to describe
Learned to listen to the pain

Maybe I need to get out
Of this godforsaken town
Where memories of him
Tend to linger around

Condescending but can't tell
Critical but you "mean well"
Statuesque, stoic hero that fell
You're in ruins,
now a cynical shell

I've clung hard to my youth
You know it's hard to face
the truth
Aged out of your same excuse
What is there left to do?
You tore me down at my best
At my worst couldn't handle me
Pacing, asking the question
Where is there left to be?

But I'll stop blaming you
for all my problems
'Cause I know that won't ever
solve them
Finally knock you off your
pedestal
So things you say don't hurt
like they used to

Retribution

Lost myself in the fire
I should've learned
What that kind of destruction
Can do to someone

Smelled of ashes for the longest time
Burned from flames
Bursting from my heart
Healing, but I can't let go
Of dark places I still call home

Grief has threaded into my bones
Brittle and woven thick with vines
The kind of complicated that to remove
Can take your whole life

Collapsed from the fatigue
From fighting myself
My enemies are gone
So what is left?

Fruitless

Lush red lips
And a heart meant for breaking
I bit into you
Like you were for the taking
Bitter to the taste
Poisoned and laced
Juice dripping from my chin
Knew from that moment
You were a walking sin
Pretending I didn't notice

The hunger crept up in me
You could never give me what I need
Got a pit in my stomach
When I saw you to the core
Feasted on the flesh
But always wanting more
Guess I paid the price
An eternity for my vice

Plucked you from the tree
Should've just let you be
Such a beautiful facade
But nothing underneath
My sacrifice was useless
This union was fruitless

Ivory

The sting of rejection
The bite of the truth
Gnaws away at your insides
Leaves you nothing to prove
I guess it knows the taste of your soul better than you do

Flesh falls away
Until you see ivory
All I keep fearing
Is that it wants more of me

So I patch all the places
Where I took the most hits
I muscle through all the unbearable moments
But I fear I've nothing left to give
Exposed and bare-boned
Can't erase the life I've already lived
It's threaded into my soul
I fear it will swallow me whole

But God help it if it attempts
My flesh may be thin
But my bones are dense

The Idea of Me

Unrealistic terms
Expectations never learned
Were we both to blame?

Now we're in a stalemate
We care but can't relate
Unwilling to change

Voluntarily in purgatory
I choose to stay
Though I can leave

You say theoretically
I'm your biggest fantasy
I'm your type aesthetically
But I just don't feel seen
Guess you only like the idea of me

Suffocating slowly
From promises
That you never keep

Feeding a growing disdain
And the river dividing
Runs too deep

Lost in a purgatory
I know I can't stay
But I don't know how to leave

Your Era Is Over

Time spent daydreaming of you
Of what we could be, what we could do
Rosy lens, our light reflected through
Warped my view of the truth

Refracted and broken
Our love forever soaked in
History's darkest moments
Left with emotions to work through

The universe seems senseless
Was brought here just as a witness
To stand trial for the sin of wanting to be with you
I just wanted to be with you

I hear people always say
History repeats unless you change
But old eras seem to bleed into
Cycles just as they start anew

Every revelation
Comes from rehabilitation
From the romanticization
Of everything we once knew

But your era is over
Broken but I will recover
From my blinding desire
To only be with you
I thought I wanted to be with you

I time travel through moments
You know I'd rather just forget
A need for self-preservation
But letting go comes in phases
And I'm still letting go of you
Even though our time is through
I'm still letting go of you

Histrionics

Trusting souls precariously cuffed by sordid partners
I watched nervously as they all fall asunder
I bite away at all my nails
I bite my tongue and bide my time

What a sad display of histrionics
Who knew loneliness could be so chaotic
I spent so long thinking I could fight it
I hate that it's all I wanted

I was never one for dramatics
I didn't want the spotlight
You held me back
Made me the Bonnie to your Clyde

What a sad display of histrionics
Who knew loneliness could be so chaotic?
Whatever you were selling I guess I bought it
I hate that you were what I wanted

Desperate times call for desperate measures
Living life at other people's pleasure
Is this what I stand for?
A supine soul fulfilled by nothing more
Than romantic gestures
Covering the worst intentions

It's a sad display of histrionics
Loneliness can be so chaotic
I hate that it's all I wanted

Emerald

I didn't become a woman when I met you
I was a girl adorned in paint, oils, and jewels
Splashed on a canvass with no clear image
A painful way to exist
Knowing I could be something that made sense

I put on the necklace that you gave me
You know how I used to like to pretend
But as the years pressed on
My love for you became contempt

The world is always waging
A war against aging
But wisdom is underrated
For it is in wisdom I found
A possession so profound
A treasure coveted
By even those wearing crowns

I didn't become a woman when I met you
I became a woman when I met myself

Split Second

Quivering breath
No respect
Bite my tongue
Words better kept
If my breath is heavy
I'd rather be running instead

One earring beside the bed
I considered it for a moment
But the moment left
With every word I wept

Split-second discernment
A union lacking purpose
Sometimes I think I deserve it
If I relax, will I enjoy it?

Dam the flood
It's a party now
I'll show my teeth
I'm ready for the crowd
But you better bow down

Washed Up

Overextended myself
Paying cab fare to your apartment
Washed up on your front porch
Desperate and guarded

Swirling crystalline pieces
In amber liquor
Light flickers across your face
Eyes light up, I sip quicker

Blow through your door
Stretch out over your bed
Crying because I'm somewhere
I don't want to be again

You wanted in
I'm sorry I can't pretend
To be the person
That you think that I am

Clinging to something not for me
Just another night of revelry
In a city that used to feel like home
It's really starting to get old

Tenderness

A haze of tenderness
Suffused throughout my torso
Weak hands and a sudden
increase in blood flow
Delicate vision
The sharpest precision
Nervously quiet
But no indecision

I knew it was you
It was always, always going to be you
It is you
It is always, always going to be you

Pierced right through the veil
That I've spent years weaving
Went right to the wound
Stopped all the bleeding
There's nothing I can do
I knew it was you

Stumbled through words so much
I forgot to mention
I'm in the middle of
A second reinvention
Not sure where I'll land
Or who I will be
But I know one thing with certainty

That it is you
It is always, always going to be you
It is you
It is always, always going to be you

Began to fall in love with
The part of me that I hated
Softened my soul
To emerald from being jaded
There's nothing I can do
It was always, always going to be you

December

Perched up in the front seat
Thinking on beat
If I like this song
Will you like me?

Frigid outside and in
Still I climbed the mountain
You can't get me out of my head
Guess I should've known then

You were angry at me
For not carrying a conversation
But we speak the same language
And my words still require a
translation

Placed your hand gently on my
torso
And I ripped it away
You couldn't let me be
You had to fill up the space

Psychoanalyzing my relationship
with my father
Funny I could've asked you
why you don't
spend Christmas with
your mother

Bright red when you beat me
at my games
God, you won't let me have
anything
But I'm not all innocent
There are some things
that I regret

Adorning your tree
Drinking too much for me
Presence never fit comfortably
But anyway I won't remember
in the morning

Strung beads awkwardly across
the branches
You asked me why
I told you I wanted something
For you to remember me by

Specter

It's the fog on the windshield
As we're driving through snow

It's the breath that you let out
Thinking I wouldn't know

It's the gray in the sky
When it can't make up its mind

It's the warmth of your body
As you slip out a lie

It's the dance before dusk
And the morning alone

It's missing the comfort
While being at home

It's burning your lips
While loving the taste

It's something you crave
That always slips away

It's the specter of soul
While present in body

It's quieting yourself
For the benefit of somebody

Frozen

Suspended above my body
Hovering over like a daydream
Mood's got me down again
Wishing I wasn't me

Fossilized in an hourglass
With time still flying past
Seems like everyone's living their life
It's just never felt like my time

Freezing to death
In a mountainous tundra
I've been walking through
Since I can remember

My strongest fear
The one that lingers in the dark
Is not knowing when I leave
If anyone will care who I was

Vines climbing a marble statue
Of some great leader
No one can relate to
But it had me thinking
Whether success is truly a virtue

Winter Rain

It's depressing
The lack of snow
Even the weather doesn't know
How to be cold
I miss the quiet of the snowfall
And shoving flakes from my coat

It's no wonder that I came home
It's the only place that knows me
to the bone
'Cause it's just like me
Yeah, it's just like me
It doesn't know how to be cold

Cure

I tried to outrun the sadness
Spent the summer out West
Drinking whiskey by the ocean
The Pacific baptized again

Living in the moment
Ignoring all your texts
You told me you'd leave me alone
This narrative's getting old

It's back and forth, back and forth
Till I run out of words to say
I'm too tired of
Always having to negotiate
You're in damage control
Don't you think you're a little late?
I thought you were my cure
But you're just more of the same

I learned to embrace the doubt
Decided to move to the South
Went to find my roots again
Buried myself in the garden

Blooms delayed with the drought
But I've learned my lesson now
Wrongs will never make a right
It's wisdom as old as time

I moved to the city
Expecting I'd lose the old me
Went to blonde from brunette
Traded my bare feet for stillets
Ran around this town
Looked for love everywhere
That it would never be found

It was always back and forth,
back and forth
Till I ran out of words to say
I was too tired of
Always having to negotiate
Now I'm in damage control
Praying that I'm not too late
I thought you were my cure
But you were just more of the same

Morning Notes (It Was Just a Dream)

I fell asleep last night with you on my mind
Went into a dream with a picture of a former life
I've really gotta stop talking about what was
'Cause I get sick of hearing myself talk about us

I dreamed that I was right by your side
You said you'd be back in the morning this time
When you didn't it wasn't you I was mad with
It was myself for letting you in again
I woke up in a cold sweat, tears running down my face
Afraid 'cause I don't want to go back to that place

You're a nostalgic resident of my mind
Why do bad memories get sweeter with time
There's something beautiful about tragic love
Maybe it's the longing or maybe it's that
Reveling in pain keeps expectations low
'Cause at least then you'll always know
And it feels good in this chaotic life being in control

Letter to a Former Lover

You'd hardly recognize me
Blonde hair, expensive perfume
Heels pounding the pavement
A little more damaged
But wiser nonetheless
Hope you're somewhere nice
At peace with your past

Our happy ever after
Was just a single chapter
In a story I'm still writing
Remember our dreams of coffee shops
In the Northwest
An indie hipster fantasy
Not knowing by December if we would last

Remember all the people we buried
By nineteen I was so sick of death
Losing you felt like the end
Yet it was like taking another breath

God, I didn't know anything
I was just a kid
Don't hold it against me
You know I never did

Do you miss those days?
Living in a tropical suburbia
I hope you think of those moments
In between all the rest

Cloister

Roaming through the open air
Breezing through these
hallowed halls
Like a wandering apparition
coming
Home after hearing a call

I recognize the place I love
And now I frequently exalt
The place I left so long ago
And blamed for all my faults

I thought this was my prison
Turns out freedom
can be seclusion
Left for the open ocean
To manifest all my delusions

I trace the stone along the wall
Fingers drawing an infinity
Found out that nothing is quite
What it seems to be

Looking at how far I've come
Feels like it was just a day before
That I tore up all those love letters
And finally closed the door

Spirit has a funny way
Of making you learn your lesson
The water isn't always clearer
On the other side of the basin

Summertime, palm trees
Mediterranean dream
Whispers of you came
Calling back to me

The allure of the unknown
Made its way out of my mind
Now all I crave is that kind
Of seclusion all the time

Sleepless Beauty

You sit all alone
In your cozy prison
You won't let me in
Or tell me how you're feeling
But I know solace can be
The first step to healing

You're beautiful and oh so kind
Someone told you once
You were just a star in the sky
I'm here to tell you not to
believe that lie

Statuesque and stoic
You're my hero and
You don't even know it
You slay all your demons
And you do it alone
You know you don't even
need them
You shine on your own

So many people in this world
It's hard to believe
That you matter at all
But you matter to me

So on those nights
When you can't seem to sleep
When something doesn't feel right
And you start to believe
That the skeletons in your closet
Are more than just a dream
You should know
Not everything is as it seems

Highlight Reel

Stuck in a loop, scrolling through a past life
Is it bad to say I miss the glory from that time?
God, I hope that's not my only highlight

A triumphant win in a challenging feat
I exchange war stories in an effort to please
But deep down I'm hoping there's more to me

Collective fear of falling short
Unlocked through constant reminders
Of "what's mine isn't yours"

A perpetual fear that I'm missing something
Am I missing something?

It's hard going against the grain
I do it time and time again
And I never know if it's the right thing

Don't listen to people when they say
"Why'd you leave?"
God, no, why'd you stay?

When there's nothing left for you
Move on without second-guessing
Just follow your instinct

Aura

Isn't it ironic how those things that never made sense
Were what saved me from my darkest moments?
When I faced the final reckoning
All I had left was me
My faith fell into your hands
Cried out, begging for another chance

Everyone has their savior
Just as everyone has their vice
Both of them can help you
Sleep through the night
But tangibility burns out like a cigarette
And withdrawal cuts like a knife

A specter, an aura
That courses through your veins
A fog settling on the shore
Colors dancing after it rains
A peaceful hum that rings
Throughout your brain
You tap into it and feel
Everything

Sun-Shower

I'm in this awkward phase
It barely shines, it barely rains
Healing isn't linear
That's what they say

But all the highs and lows
And all the places I used to go
Don't feel the same
They don't feel the same

I walk in the shadows
But every now and then
I see the cracks
So I run a little faster
But I know it won't work
like that

You asked me how I've been today
I'm honestly afraid to say
It changes every single minute
And one thought can put me in it

I walk in the shadows
But every now and then
I see the cracks
So I relish in the moment
'Cause I know that's all we have

I found you
It's still a mood
Any little joys
I'll lean into
All the in-betweens
I won't let them get to me
The sun covered every other hour
Can make fleeting feelings
Feel like a sun-shower

Wildflower

Wildflower, you're still brand new
Got this whole life in front of you
Yellow, green, and so many different hues
Things are always messy when they're true

And I've spent so many hours
Lying in the grass
Dreaming of a world beyond where I am at
All the days just flying past
Stuck in my mind

It's all right
Forgive yourself for
The time that you've wasted
On people and places
That you've outgrown

Expectations never quite
Meet you where you're at
But they catch up eventually
I can guarantee that

And you've got so much time, Wildflower
To grow

The Hardest Thing

I played a part
I was certainly naive
Maybe had tunnel vision
With the lies I started to believe
But I knew it was wrong
And that I hurt you
For that I must atone
And recognize two things can be true

So I'm on my knees
Saying I'm sorry
I'm sorry
I'm sorry
I'm sorry

Taking a step back without
Going over the cliff
Proved to be the hardest thing
I'll do while I exist
To self-correct without the shame
Proved to be the hardest thing
The hardest thing

I don't need your forgiveness
I wouldn't ask you to give it
But it's hard living
Knowing I left a permanent imprint
That will weave its way into every facet of your life
That can only be washed away with time
That's what keeps me up at night

This is the last time I'll think about you
And all the hell I put you through
Because it's torture every time that I do
But if I want to stay in this life
I have to close this chapter and leave it behind
I would take it all back if I could
To save us from the pain we endured

So
I'm sorry
I'm sorry
I'm sorry
Self-correcting without the shame
Proved to be the hardest thing
The hardest thing

Resurrection

Resurrection lies in forgetting about your past
Starve the shame so you know it can't last
Subjecting yourself to penance
Guarantees your mistakes will become a life sentence

Taught to question ourselves
By those who don't know
They watch in the arena
But can't feel the breath of the bull
And I'm so sick to my stomach
Of caring that I don't care at all

I've seen the best of the best get swallowed whole by shame
I've seen people with the worst intentions
Get excused for a lot more
The universe has a cruel way of balancing things
Atone, get out, and let yourself be reborn

If you decide you want to do better
People will change with you
Shed your skin and don't ever settle
For what you think you deserve
You have a long life to live
But you only have one

The Seeker

Took a walk and scared myself
Realized the water was deeper than the well
All my fears inside left me paralyzed
But the seeker can never tell

The heat of the moment
May have left me heated and broken
But for every time I've given up
I've also answered the call
So now I'll lean into the fall